Joe the Barber's

100 GRASSROOTS CAMPAIGN STRATEGIES

Voice of the People"

www.trafford.com

North America & international
toll-free: 1 888 232 4444 (USA & Canada)
phone: 250 383 6864 ♦ fax: 812 355 4082

100 Campaign Strategies for political success is a proven guide for a successful political campaign for first time candidates and veterans of political wars. A must do for eliciting favorable voters and volunteers. Joe takes you from your declaration of candidacy to get out the voter (GOTV) on Primary and Election Day. For over a half century Joe has directed and participated in advancing political campaigns of candidates for local, state and federal elections.

Grassroots campaigns are the voice of the people, the voice of your voters and an energized movement to motivate volunteers & voters.

I guarantee that the candidate who uses my Grassroots Campaign has the best chance to win the election. Before candidates used their contributions for enormous media campaigns there was grassroots campaigning, the candidate and his volunteers. It about meeting the voters and all politics is local. Trust me; I will get you more votes with Grassroots Campaigning.

For over 55 years Joe Muschiano

Has Directed and Participated in the 100 strategies & tactics that have advanced the political campaigns of candidates for local, state and federal elections.

Feature Article in Rhode Island Monthly November 1996

Since I was in my teens, I've been involved in politics -- four decades. My father was a barber and a political animal. I learned politics in his barber shop. I shined shoes there when I was seven and started learning barbering when I was eleven. I got my barbering license when I was fourteen, and I still work in the shop weekends.

I got interested in politics from my dad, but I was never into running as a candidate. When I was twenty-one, my father says the future wave was Republican and I think it was, until Nixon screwed up. So I checked it out. The Republicans wanted me. I was a young Italian Catholic and they could count the numbers of those they had on one hand. I came back to my father and I said I can't. They're not my kind of people, they were Swamp Yankees. I first became famous on the Buddy Cianci talk radio show. I would talk to Buddy almost daily. I presented him with the Outstanding Talk Show Host of the Year "Award in 1990. We've been friends ever since,

I wrote Election Strategies: How to Find'em and Vote'em in the 1990s, because I was looking for a basic book on political strategies and there weren't any. It's being sold all over the country. It's been picked up by Brown Bookstore.

In politics, I've leaned loyalty is the most important thing. Governor Bruce Sundlun asked me to help him with his campaign, by then, I was a celebrity on talk radio. I said I would and I, with others on talk radio, led the march of five thousand volunteers to the Sundlun camp for the 1990 campaign.

I'm the voice of the average guy on the street. This month we're going to have Reed as senator, Weygand as congressman, and Kennedy's re-election and you can take that to the bank. And any jerk knows Clinton's going to win because of Newtie and his fruities and the Christian Coalition. The Republicans have scared the hell out of everybody.

Why should people listen to me? Because I speak from the heart, and who can't identify with the local barber?

Formal Education

- Rhode Island College 1992: Master in Art of History.
- Thomas A Cooley Law School 1986: Lansing Michigan: JD Law program: Contracts 1, Criminal Law and Property.
- Rhode Island College 1985: Bachelor of Liberal Arts, Concentration in Political Science.
- Community College of Rhode Island 1983: Associate in Business Administration.

R I State Government Experience

- November 1995 to2004: Protective Service Officer (Substance Abuse Specialist), Department of Elderly Affairs, and State of Rhode Island

- September 1993 to August 1995: Substance Abuse Administrator, Department of Substance Abuse, and State of Rhode Island

- Client Advocacy; For most clients I was the person of last resort. I facilitated client treatment and attempted to resolve conflict between the clients and the treatment programs and the State Bureaucracy. Treatment programs included; inpatient, outpatient, methadone detoxification and maintenance, and residential and/or follow up treatment.

- Monitoring: I developed policy and procedure for the monitoring of the Student Assistance Programs, four agencies and fifty-nine schools.

Policy Analyst for Public Safety Departments
Governor Bruce Sundlun's Executive Staff
State of Rhode Island

September 1991 to 1993
Legislation and Budget Analyst: All related duties for:
- Department of Substance Abuse
- Department of Corrections
- Departments of Public Safety
- Municipal Police and Fire, State Police, Governor's Department of Highway Safety and the Governor's Justice Commission.
- Developed data for a proposed Department Of Public Safety.

CONTENTS

I'll show you how to

Chapter One
Staff to Win on the Campaign Trail
- How to Organize
- Name Recognition to Build Your Brand
- Frontrunner in 13-Steps
- Field Director & Advance Team
- Donors in 5-level
- True Story of Name Recognition Tactics
- Campaign Promotion Materials
- Story of my winning volunteer recruitment campaign.

Be a creditable candidate in short time and money you will capture the imagination of the voters. Strategies are outlined for campaign handouts, materials and events and directs where to go, what to do and how to do it. I will direct your organization's strategies for the *campaign trail* and *in-house.*

You will partner your name recognition with your brand as the Front runner in 13-steps. And formulate your organization in-house staff complimented by a field organization. *I'll show you how to get donations from 5-levels of donors.* I include a true story of Name Recognition Tactics and My winning volunteer recruitment campaign.

Become a creditable candidate and capture the imagination of the voters in a short period of time with minimal capital. Learn how to direct your organization's campaign strategies "in-house" with Handouts/Flyers, Materials, Events, and step by step instructions on what to do, where to do it and how to do it.

Partner your name recognition with your brand as the front runner in 13 easy to follow steps. Compliment your in-house organization strategies with those in the field and learn how to secure contributions from 5-Levels of contributors.

Pave the Road to Victory! VOLUNTEERS * VOLUNTEERS and more VOLUNTEERS is what will prove to be the deciding factor who wins the election. For Primary Day 3000 volunteers were in every precinct in the State for the unendorsed candidate for Governor. On General Election Day 5,000 volunteers moved the campaign. We won our Primary! A true story of how it works.

Chapter Two
Win Your Primary

- Cultivate your base
- Identify your Favorable & Volunteers to increase your vote.
- Your Undecided & Independents Vote
- Identify the Party's Base
- Target the Party's Faithful
- Survey to rate you & your opponent
- Target 5 groups of potential supporters
- Measure Persuadable & Performances
- Opposition Research the Opposition's Vote & Plan
- Know your Enemy
- Identify Your Donors
- GOTV a database of Favorables, volunteers and other potential supporters

In chapter 2 you will cultivate your base by identifying your favorable/volunteers. The Undecided & Independents Vote will increase your vote. As a party candidate you will identify your Party's base, target the Party's faithful, target 5 groups of your potential supporters, measure persuadable & performances and a survey to rate you & your opponent. GOTV a database of Favorable, volunteers and other potential supporters. Opposition Research to know your challenges and your Donors

Chapter Three
GOTV Election Week & Day
- ID faster, more actuate.
- Motivate Volunteers & Favorable.
- Light up the district for Election.
- GOTV Favorable IDs
- Checker Plan to Win
- Tracking with Voter Par Count

Light up the district for the election is a must. You will ID faster, more actuate and motivate Favorable that will bring on volunteers. As you GOTV Favorable IDs using your volunteers to Check-off the voters you will be able to track how the vote is going with my Voter Par tracking. An Election Day situation demonstrates how GOTV was accomplished to save the Primary Election.

My true story of how I directed a Senatorial Primary Election in the last 3 hours to save a win. This is what it's all about... I will direct you to what must be done to motivate the campaign & light up the district for Election Day. Your volunteers will vote the Favorable and execute a masterful GOTV.

**How to Organize
A Grassroots Organization**

CHAPTER ONE

I'll show you how to

Staff to Win on the Campaign Trail
- How to Organize
- Name Recognition to Build Your Brand
- Frontrunner in 13-Steps
- Field Director & Advance Team
- Donors in 5-level
- True Story of Name Recognition Tactics
- Campaign Promotion Materials
- Story of my winning volunteer recruitment campaign.

Your "Staff to Win" organization will be the campaign's promoters on the campaign trail and in house. You need a headquarters & staff that have a Grassroots-Campaign agenda to carry out the dozens of strategies and tactics that will bring you to an Election Day victory. Headquarters: It's Location, Location where there is high visibility and easily accessible.

You need a HQ that will have high visibility and easily accessible on the ground floor in the middle of town's main street or in a strip mall. Heavy traffic and people movement is a must. You want a very active HQ that will show that you have a solid organization and enthusiastic volunteers. This HQ situation is inviting to the voters to walk in.

<u>Campaign HQ Sign</u>

CANDIDATE'S NAME
Picture It's the Economy
POLITICAL OFFICE
www.cname@blank.com

The HQ windows & sign should have inviting pertinent information. Adopt a campaign symbol for a window display. This format is always recommended for other campaign signs.

- The candidate's name & office he is running for
- The party he wants to represent
- Picture of the candidate
- Include the website on all signs and literature.

The Organization & Initial HQ campaign staff

Start the campaign with an Office Person who can do multiple jobs until you need more staff. You may be able to utilize volunteers.

- office manager
- receptionist
- scheduler
- volunteer coordinator
- Field Director
- Communication Director

Communication Director

The Communication Director is in charge of public appearances press releases -TV-Cable-Radio. The spoke person for the campaign he will keep you out of harms way. He needs to make sure the advance team has what is needed for any media situation for the day.

The Scheduling Calendar

Place the campaign's scheduling calendar on line. This will show the voters and supporters how active the campaign is. Place a second calendar on line for the campaign staff and volunteers to know where to be and when.

Website

Have a website up & running for the day you declare your candidacy. Declare you're a candidate and release your campaign plan. Your press release and plan should be sent by e-mail to all your supporters and media outlets.

Keep your supporters in the loop on you're Website

- Obtain voter response
- Posting videos
- A way for voters to donate

Encourage potential supporter to get on board and volunteer. Post an invitation for *Coffee Times* with the candidate on a regular basis. I suggest every last Wednesday of the month from 6:30 p m to 7:00 p m. Encourage supporters & volunteers to bring at least one voter to the coffee hour.

All press releases are placed on the Web. The candidate's position on issues is available. The Candidates Plan is about the main issue(s) the voters are concerned about. "The Smith Plan"

Database

The Advance Team will bring in the names of potential supporters. The In House staff must set up a database to identify the voters contacted in the field. Database files of supporters, Favorable, Volunteers, Undecided & voters who have the greatest potential to support you. Every contact is a possible donor. Every Contact is included in the Email Letters. Every voter meeting on the campaign trail should receive a follow-up call.

Field Director - Advance Team

The field director is the point man for the candidate. He and the advance team travels with the candidate and advance his appearances. You are on the Campaign Trail with the Field Director, Advance Team, volunteers, community and political leaders. A Team's priority on the campaign trail is to find potential supporters and obtain as many phone numbers and Emails as possible. Local leaders should participate in their respective precincts with advance team members.

- Everyone should wears hats, stickers and distribute literature.
- The candidate should always ask every voter for his support and if he believes he may have it, ask for the voter to be a volunteer.
- You will meet thousands on the campaign trail. If you and Team collected business cards, phone numbers & emails you have your target groups for your database.
- Yes business cards. That is the first thing you ask the voters. It's quicker, easier & complimentary way to get phone numbers & emails
- You have distributed Slim Jims and Volunteer Action Committee VAC Packs to Family Friends & Neighbors (FF&N).

Politics 101: put the candidate with the people and enhances his presence with literature and enthusiastic volunteers.

1. Prepare the candidate for events. Prepare everything the candidate will need for the events of the day. Have the right and appropriate literature and other campaign materials for the events.
2. Always have Press Kits on hand for the media. Locate the media and prepare them for the candidate's coming.
3. The candidate's time is valuable. The Team must find the best route in and out. Locate the best place for the candidate to enter the event.
4. Have the local dignitaries there to greet him. Have local volunteers, political and community leaders to introduce him to the voters.
5. The best way to get volunteers is for the candidate's Advance Team to solicit the voters on the campaign trail. When traveling with the candidate the team should observe and listen to the voters the candidate talks to. The Team will hear the voters who support him and others who show an interest in him. Get their info. May I have your business card?"
6. As the candidate moves on to one voter after another, Team members should ask for the following information:

1-Business Card &

2-Name _____ E-mail _____

Address _____ Tel # home_____ work_____ cell_____

If I am doing Advance for a candidate I will increase his votes by thousands. I never miss a potential volunteer. Make sure your Team members are people oriented. In a campaign a team can sign up and find potential volunteers who will bring in more volunteers.

A Grassroots campaign is all about having committed voters, supporters and active volunteers sign-up.

Literature

Remember your literature has an invitation to become a volunteer and an invite to the campaign's headquarters Coffee Times every 4th Wednesday night. This is very important to voters, availability and accessibility of the candidate.

At the coffee hours encourage voters to take home a yard sign, bumper stickers and VAC Packs to distribute to Family Friends & Neighbors (FF&N).

Suggested VAC Pack campaign items

Distribute Slim Jims and Volunteer Action Committee VAC Packs for FF&N on the trail.

1. Slim Jim Handouts and/or 3-Fold Flyers
2. Letter to voters from volunteers asking for their support (Create a letter and have the volunteers write in the voter's name and signed by the volunteer.)
3. Sticker – Lapel and bumper
4. Ballot placement of the candidate (when it is determined)
5. Campaign materials that will help the **voter decide for the candidate.**

3-fold flyer:

A 3-fold flyer gives voters a look at the candidate from different perspectives using pictures to show the business man, the community involved man, the man on the campaign trail. Be creative. Promote the brand.

1. The flyer should contain a section that highlights the main issues of the campaign and the candidate's position.

2. Ask voters to go to your website and register their e-mails for your e-mail letters. You want them informed of all press releases and your position on issues.

3. Have a section in the flyer to encourage voters to sign up, call, or email to be a volunteer, for a yard sign and a bumper sticker.

4. A letter to the voters asking for their support and why you believe it's in their best interest to do so.

5. An invitation for the Coffee Times. Encourage volunteers to bring at least one voter to the coffee hour. This could result in more volunteers who will take home VAC Packs for FF&N.

Dear _____

I am a volunteer and I want to introduce (name) (party) candidate for (office). Please accept an invitation to you, your family and friends an invitation to (candidates) headquarters every 4th Wednesday from 7:00 P.M. to 8:30 P.M. Please feel free to stop in anytime at (candidate's name) headquarters. The attached campaign flyer highlights who (candidate's name) is and the kind of (office he is running for) he will be.

_____

Sincerely, (your neighbor)
The volunteer will write in the voters name and sign their name.

Emails for Pictures

If you are running in a large district for Mayor, Senator or Congress use the Emails for photos with the candidate. It's a trade off. Have your camera man take pictures of you and voters. A team member can give the voters a card with the information he will need to retrieve the picture. The voter will have to register his Emails. You will have a random voter database to ID.

Support Groups

Have all groups that support you organize an e-mail address list of all their members. Support groups should encourage their members to participate in the Coffee Times with the candidate every 4th Wednesday every month, and bring a potential supporter. Hold a special Coffee Time if need be.

Phone Bank

- Organize a phone bank of volunteer's best to ID the Favorable
- You want an Email database; ID supporters, volunteers, Favorable, potential and undecided. I have found that many undecided were the opposition's voters.
- You want to ask all Favorable to be a volunteer. Take all prisoners.
- Invite all voters to attend the next "Coffee Time" with the candidate and inform them of the day and times every month one will be held.

Candidate's volunteer recruiting sessions

Candidates spend a lot of hours calling and soliciting donations. They have to, in order to move the donor's funds to his campaign. However he fails to spend sufficient time and effort getting volunteers interested in the workings of his campaign.

You should organize volunteer phone bank sessions where the volunteers, on multiple phones, call the Favorable and potential supporters. The callers should try to convince the voters to support the candidate and the Favorable to become a volunteer. The candidate should ask the reluctant voters to the Coffee Time so they can discuss any reservations the voter may have.

Moving from voter to voter during this process the candidate should end the conversation with the voters and thank the new volunteer for joining the campaign and hopefully to meet them at the next Coffee Time if not before.

VOLUNTEERS, VOLUNTEERS
Will prove to be the deciding factor of who wins the election.

My Story of recruiting volunteers
I was invited to candidate for Governor Bruce Sundlun's opening of his campaign headquarters. As I was standing with his staff and other supporters I was grabbed and pushed between Sundlun and his wife Marjorie. Snap went the camera. I was singled out for a picture that would be personally delivered by Sundlun to my barber shop.

I reported the next day over talk radio that there were about 300 at the meeting; a little political exaggeration. I was probably and probably still am the most noted talk show caller in Rhode Island.

I started my own grassroots volunteer movement that I personally multiplied into 750 volunteers for the campaign. Seeing how successful I was I convinced the Sundlun campaign to adopt *my volunteer recruitment campaign*. We sent out newsletters to supporters to be volunteers and to sign up volunteers.

Sundlun was the unendorsed candidate in a three way Democrat primary. By primary day we had over 3000 volunteers in every precinct in the 39 cities and towns in the State. Every volunteer was working to sign new volunteers. We defeated the endorsed candidate Providence Mayor and the unendorsed Warwick Mayor.

Ready for General Election
A professional phone bank was calling and identifying the Favorable. Every Favorable was entered in a database for a volunteer phone bank to call the Favorable and encourage them to join the campaign. By Election Day the campaign recruited over 5,000 volunteers under the direction and guide of Jean McCarthy, volunteer coordinator.

Jean was the staff person who came to my barber shop and interviewed me to join the campaign. It was her insight of my abilities to convince the Sundlun organization that I was "OK". The voice of the volunteers was heard and responded too.

Brand & Name Recognition
Having a name without a brand is like having no identity.
- Building your brand & name recognition will identify you - the candidate
- Name recognition & branding are needed to start and move a political candidate into a creditable position and in turn a credibility candidate.
- If you follow the strategies & tactics in Grassroots-Campaigning they will show you how to get out in Front. Be first out of the gate and stay in the lead to GOTV and a win.

A political campaign must ask. What are the negatives to an issue or any campaign strategy and tactic? If it has negatives avoid it. Perception is political reality. Forget the intent, its all about perception. Make sure right from the start, no negatives.

Build Your Brand with a double message.
The candidate needs a slogan that will Brand his name to give him a political identity. You the candidate, your slogan and your message make up your political identity. "Perception is Political Reality"

Your slogan should imply a negative about your opponent and a positive about yourself. If your opponent and her surroundings have an air of distrust then "Trust Me" will have a two way message and will give you the brand of trust. What the voters perceive and what you portray is political reality. Brand a two-way message

You will enhance your image and Name Recognition with a Brand that has a two-way connotation. A slogan that speaks to the voters that you will be the opposite of what they dislike most about your opponent. This is the best and most effective Brand.

Sign and or Bumper Sticker
Below is an example of sign and or bumper sticker to deliver your message. In your campaign literature you will explain your slogan and message. Or you can just imply and not hit the issue head on.

Name + slogan = Branded

CANDIDATE 2010
Picture It's the Economy
POLITICAL OFFICE
www.cname@blank.com

You're credentials are economist, businessman etc.
You're opponent is talking about other issues and has a background in medicine

Name + slogan = Branded

  Smith 2010
  People First
  Governor

You're sitting Governor is all about politics & political cronies.

How to be the front-runner

The first candidate to announce his or her candidacy is the only candidate out of the gate. First is out in front. Initially there are 13-Steps to get out in Front:

1. Be the first candidate to announce your declaration to run. Have the spotlight all to yourself as long as possible.

2. Speak to groups, go on talk shows. Hit the road with a lot of fanfare burning rubber and leather. Grassroots campaigning activities will help you stay in front. Keep the voters aware of your presents by attending every public event and do all the suggestions in this Grassroots campaign.

3. Demonstrate that you have support of political and community leaders. Have them participate in and with your *Advance Team.*

4. The sooner you demonstrate that you have a very active support group of volunteers around you the better. A display of volunteers around and with the candidate is a powerful attraction to the voters, especially the undecided contemplating joining a campaign.

5. Have a Website up & running for the day you declare your candidacy. Keep your supporters in the loop.

6. Be prepared to announce your campaign Headquarters & Staff. A HQ with high visibility and heavy activity will help to give you credibility.

7. You should announce you are a candidate and release your campaign Plan out of the box in a formal press release. "The Smith Plan" Your press release and Plan should be sent by Email to all your supporters. Keeping supporters in the loop.

8. The candidate who is seen as the unofficial spokes person of issues that affects his voters, his political party. Issue press releases presenting your position on the issues that most affect the voters. Show that you are the candidate who the voters need to replace the incumbent.

9. The candidate who receives the most negative attention from the opposition is given credibility from his opponent. Get your opponent to attack you. Get in attack mode. Throw out a line and real him in to an exchange of words. Let him push the negative and you stay positive.

10. Stay positive. Let your opponent start the negatives. Keep the good and positive focus on you.

11. Demonstrate you have substantial financial fundraising ability at reporting time. If you

can match your opponent's war chest, you level the financial playing field. You will win with Grassroots campaigning with less funding then your opponent. So hit the road with a lot of fanfare, burning rubber and leather.

12. Present your Brand before the voters and build your Brand along the way that will give you a political identity. You the candidate, your slogan and your message make up your political identity. You will be the Front-runner.

13. Independent candidates start off behind. They must implement Front-runner strategies because they look like the lone candidate without any major support. The first question everyone will ask, "How much money can you raise". "How much will you right a check for?" Its credibility you need and you have to demonstrate you have or can raise the money and have a solid organization. You the Independent candidate, more then a party candidate must implement the Front-runner strategies and all my grassroots strategies. In short time and money you will be able to come from a non-political entity to a creditable candidate who's captured the imagination of the voters.

Perception is Political Reality
Candidate > Slogan > Message > Political Identity

Advice by Buddy Cianci from the Providence Monthly November 2009

What I've learned about politics

1. Don't avoid the talk shows. Take your medicine and get it over with quickly. It's much better that way and you can move on.

2. Never allow anyone to define you. The worst mistake you can make is to have someone else define you, whether it's an opponent, a newscaster, a columnist, anybody. You have to define yourself because they'll define you on their terms, not yours.
Express your opinion.

3. If there is a news story about you that's factually inaccurate, it's your job to set the facts straight. You respond by not letting anyone lead you down a path you don't want to go down. But don't go outside the four corners of that page - in other words; don't stray beyond the story that's already out in the media.

4. If a story's negative, it's best to get out in front. If you made a mistake, admit it and move on because then it becomes less of a new story.

5. If you're running for office and your opponent is strong, try to run against an institution that people dislike, instead of running against your opponent. Run against a utility company that just raised its rates. Run against the banks - anyone the public pays monthly. Run against an institution that takes money from the public, and is normally considered unfair.

6. Stay on message. Don't give the public more information than they can digest at one time. Be repetitive. Stay on message and keep reinforcing.

7. Sometimes the key to success is opposition research. Don't be afraid to spend money on research, especially things like your opponent's voting record. If you can $500 worth of damage on a Rolls Royce in a showroom, you can find something in your opponent's record that's useful. No one's perfect.

8. If someone twists the facts about you or deliberately distorts your message, you're letting him define you. As many times as he says it, you have to repeat that it's not true. If it is true, try to change the subject.

The following campaign tactics and suggested materials will promote you, your campaign and bring aboard the supporters/volunteers needed to carry out your grassroots campaign.

- Present your Name & Brand to the Voters
- Put your message in front of the voters
- Attract volunteers and supporters
- Use all political and public events in the most effective ways outlined in my tactics to contact the voters for support
- The multiple events for promotion
- Use the *Advance Team* field organization to present the candidate.
- Use suggested material to promote the candidate and the campaign. Be created.

Campaign Promotion Materials

Slim Jims
The Slim Jims, about 4x8, should have a picture of the candidate and a brief resume, a laundry list of his background. The picture on the Slim Jim should show the candidate. One with his family is always good. The Slim Jim should fit in the shirt pocket with the picture showing. Above the picture the candidate's name and seat he is running for.

Include an invitation to the *Coffee Time* with the candidate every 4th Wednesday of the month at the HQ. This day of the month is probably the least active in voter's schedule. This is very important to voters that you are availability and accessibility. At the coffee hours you can distribute *VAC Packs* (voter action committee) to attendees to give to Friends Family and Neighbors (FF&N) plus yard signs.   Have volunteers pass out VAC Packs to FF&N and to bring at least one voter to the next coffee hour.

Headquarters contact information should include the address, phone number and the campaign's website and email Address. Use your imagination. Include something unique about you.

3-Fold Flyer
A 3-fold flyer gives the candidate a look from different perspectives (w/pictures), the businessman, community involved man, on the campaign trail, etc. It speaks to what this campaign is all about. It includes a letter asking the voters for their support and to join your campaign. It highlights why you are running and what you hope to do. This is for distribution during neighborhood walks and mailings.

Business Cards
Staff members should have business cards to identify themselves as campaign agents.

Include contact information. They can be standard campaign card which the staff member can write their name in.

Lapel Stickers
Lapel stickers are important for the advance to wear and carry to put on everyone who will wear one. The children love them.

Balloons
Balloons for kids are the best gift the Team can carry. All they have to do is give them to the kids and place a sticker on them and they have won the parent's attention. During parades and festivals you can distribute balloons flying in the air with strings. Other times it may not be practical. A Balloon is a balloon to a kid even if they have to blow it up themselves.

On the Campaign Trail

Your Voter Contact Strategies started with your Name Recognition Campaign. You're out in the district meeting the voters and building your Brand. Your second priority on the campaign trail will be to get as many phone numbers and email addresses as possible.

Business Cards
Collecting business cards is the fastest way to get the information about the voter. All phone numbers and email addresses should be turned into the campaign's headquarters after each field event. The headquarters' Phone Bank and Email Campaign will contact the voters. Your email campaign will keep the voters in the loop.
The Advance Team
Politics 101: put the candidate with the people and enhances his presence with literature and enthusiastic volunteers.

Every voter meeting on the campaign trail should receive a follow-up call. "Can I include you as a supporter for _____?" The Favorable expressing interest in the candidate should receive a follow-up call and encouraged to join the campaign as a supporter. The most enthusiastic volunteers are the ones that walk in or call HQ.

Fairs/Festivals/parades and public events Campaigning

1. Parades:
- Do not march in the parades. Start out early and walk in front of the parade shaking every hand you can. Get to know the voters. *"All politics is local"*.
- Get local political and community leaders to walk with you and introduce you.
- Have a balloon team just in front of you to bring the kids running for balloons. Give a kid a balloon and put a sticker on him and her.
- Get your team in minstrel hats, T-shirts and passing out promotional literature. Have them around you to draw attentions to you.
- Demonstrate a loud presence of an enthusiastic volunteer organization. You will be the main event before the spectacular parade. Never miss a parade.

2. Fairs/festivals:
- Deliver the same excitement (parade campaign) around you at the fairs. Get the voter's attention as you walk to meet the voters.
- Set up a booth at a one-day festival or weeklong festivals to be viewed by thousands. It will be like bringing your campaign headquarters to the voters with volunteers, political and community leaders to promote you.
- Demonstrate a loud presence of an enthusiastic volunteer organization. Never miss a festival. "All politics is local."

3. The Business Walk: Main Street USA
The candidate must meet main street business owners, staff and customers and do the following tactics:
1. Walk every main street section in every county. "All politics is local"
2. Meet every business person and their patrons
3. Walk with community and political leaders
4. Meet with the news media in the area
5. Interview with a talk show in every area
6. An Advance Team person or two & volunteers too
7. Advance team distributes handouts to voters
8. An emphasis on an invitation to Coffee Times with the candidate should be made to all to come.
9. Get every Email Address & Telephone number you can.

4. Honks & Waves
Target the intersections in the district that has the busiest traffic during the commuting hours from 7:00 a. m. to 9:00 a. m. and the afternoon hours from 4:00 p. m. to 6:00 p. m. Where it is suitable, make it a day in the area for your Business & Neighborhood Walks.

Volunteers should display campaign signs and wave at the motorist. Use campaign signs with your picture. Remember your team is in minstrel hats, T-shirts and passing out promotional Slim Jims and 3-Fold flyers when ever possible.

Honk & Wave in the A.M. and have breakfast in a local restaurant (an area business). Move on and campaign main street businesses until lunch. After lunch continue canvassing until 4:00 P. M. Stop in all barbershops, beauty shops, real-estate offices, and all other local owned business. Use your Slim Jims and 3-Fold flyers.

Your Advance Team should be drawing attention to you and collecting names telephone numbers and Emails of all who show an interest. (See HQ & Staff)

5. The Neighborhood Walk
Family Friends & Neighbor's Campaign promotes the candidate to FF&N and demonstrates a big presence in the neighborhoods. Volunteers with hats & t-shirts distribute literature to FF& N. During the walks with the candidate volunteers should ask the voters if they care to meet the candidate.

6. City & Town employee visits
Make a special effort to visit all police and fire departments, city and town halls and all other municipal building and meet the public servants that will likely vote in the elections. It is best, but not necessary to have a local escort who knows most of the employees.

Billboards are great. You're before the voters every hour of every day. Also rolling billboards are even better and cheaper. Get Pickup trucks and big box trucks and put signs and banners on them.

Measure the Persuadable & Performances

You need to receive the greatest return for your campaign efforts. Determine the precincts that will return you the most votes for your campaign's efforts.

- What are the precincts that you should spend more time doing Business Walks, Neighborhood Walks and Honks & Waves?
- Where you should get your supporters out with VAC Packs to FF&N?

In 2006 in precinct #1 the vote for the Senate Candidate was 2,000 votes more then the Congressional Candidate of the same party. The difference between the Congressional Candidate and the Mayoral Candidate in the same precinct was close. The voters liked the Mayoral and Congressional candidates about equal. The same voters like the Senate candidate 2,000 votes more then the Congressional candidate. This precinct has the possibility of 2,000 persuadable voters.

You will find precincts that are consistent in their voting habits over the past two and three elections. Their voting history is a prediction for the next election. Make your appearance in the precincts that have the greatest history of independent voting.

You need to know what the percentage of the voters will turnout to vote. History of the last two elections will give you one presidential election and one non presidential election. Therefore if you are running in a non presidential year you have to use the last two non presidential elections as a guide.

You should find the voters who voted in the last presidential election and missed the previous non presidential election. Those voters should be identified to see if they are persuadable.

"A True Story of Name Recognition Tactics"

Name Recognition &
Make claim to the party's nomination for the next election

In 1994 a Democrat campaign victory for Rhode Island General Treasure was a long shot. Nancy Mayer was the popular Republican incumbent and the rule of thumb is the electorate fire incumbents, they do not hire challengers. Therefore, it follows that the electorate will not hire a political unknown to replace a popular incumbent who has a positive public image. Then why run if it's hopeless? For 2 reasons: Name recognition and to claim the nomination for next election's open seat.

Polling gave the Democratic candidate 15%. The Democrat base was 35% to 40%. Democrat Richard James, a political unknown was way below his party's base.

Without sufficient funds to buy name recognition James found it impossible to mount an effective media campaign. Approximately $90,000 was spent on the campaign and 80 percent of that amount was spent on media.

The campaign had to rely on a grassroots campaign for name recognition and a claim on the nomination for next election's open seat. I targeted 22 of the 39 cities and towns with the greatest number of Democrats. They were the only potential to vote for a Democratic candidate. The grassroots campaign, while under-funded was successful.

The following 12 cities/towns had a heavy concentration of Democrats. We went after the Democrats base. There was no way we would get any significant Independent vote. We used literature, signs and balloons while we wore t-shirts & hats to draw attention to our candidate. While James touched the flesh of every Democrat on the campaign trail. We used all visible means getting the candidate with the voters.

- Democrat functions & political rallies
- Parades/Fairs/Festivals
- Literature drops & sign distribution
- Neighborhood and Business Walks
- GOTV visibility- reminding the Democrat voters on Election Day
- Volunteers, Volunteers and more Volunteers everyday & on Election Day

Grassroots averaged 41.9% in the top 6 cities/towns and a high of 49.5% in one. In 6 cities/towns are average was 35.5%.

In the 12 cities/towns visibility was frequent at state and local political events, before the senior citizen population and at fairs/festivals/parades; always with the advance team networking and distributing literature with local volunteers. At events that the candidate was unable to attend a literature drop was made. Also vital to the grassroots success was an area coordinator/contact person and a team of volunteers who met the advance team and walked with the candidate. The local volunteers did a Democrat voter GOTV.

Name Recognition
All politics is local even for a Presidential Primary candidate

National name recognition can be purchased; it can be won by staging performances in the form of news conferences that excite publicity, and it can be obtained by winning at the polls. Yes! You can buy it. And you can get it the way you will get the most return for your efforts; By Grassroots Campaigning.

When the former Governor of Georgia Jimmy Carter went to Iowa the polls showed that he had national name recognition of only 2%. Carter needed the Democrat Primary wins in Iowa, New Hampshire and Florida to prove he was a viable candidate by primary.

Carter's campaign strategy, a win in Iowa and New Hampshire and get the name recognition he needed to become a viable candidate. By winning in Iowa and New Hampshire meant Carter now had the momentum going into Massachusetts to win. Unfortunately his campaign was not ready with an election day GOTV. Henry "Scoop" Jackson won that day because his organization had the ability to GOTV his votes in a snowstorm. The Jackson people identified their potential favorables and with enough volunteers got them to the polls.

What Carter did effectively to become a viable candidate and obtain name recognition was to set up grassroots campaigns in every town and city in the states where he would enter as a primary candidate. By winning in Iowa, New Hampshire, and Florida, Carter created name recognition of a candidate who can win the Party's nomination.

The Iowa Plan
The Carter campaign organized the "Iowa Carter for President Steering Committee". The campaign opened 20 field offices to execute 20 separate grassroots movements. With 20 steering committee coordinators and volunteers, the Carter people were able to successfully execute targeting, networking, and GOTV.

Eleven months before the January caucus, Carter launched a 21- day campaign. He did networking strategies like handshaking on the streets and shopping centers and stood at factory gates to tell people who he was and what he was doing in Iowa.

He would send handwritten notes to people he spoke to while campaigning. If nobody was home when he went door to door he would leave a handwritten note that he had been there. He would stay in ordinary folks' homes as he drove from town to town. He won the Iowa folks over by networking them in their homes, work places and shopping areas.

More than 50,000 Iowans went to the polls and 14,000 voted for Carter. Winning Iowa gave Carter recognition he needed to show that he was a viable candidate.

New Hampshire Primary

New Hampshire was a cold winter of work for the Carter organization and the small army of volunteers from New Hampshire and Georgia. New Hampshire was like Iowa: the Carter people had the ability to make voter contact and execute an all-out effort of targeting, networking and GOTV compared to the rest of the field of candidates. They visited just about every store, barber shop, beauty parlor and restaurant. Like Iowa, New Hampshire residents were receptive to the Carter family's personal campaign style his grassroots organization of volunteers.

The Carter campaign's Georgia to New Hampshire Operation brought 90 volunteers to New Hampshire to campaign for five days. The volunteers contacted 95% of the Democratic houses (Democratic primary voters) and carried out a successful Post Card Plan. In this plan, everyone they met was sent a personal post card from the volunteer about the meeting and a reminder to vote for Carter.

Funding the Campaign

There are multiple donor groups for your campaign.
You enter the race and set the stage for Front-runner position. You're out of the gate early so everyone watches your moves. As long as you're on you're way in accomplishing the above strategies you can move to solicit donations.

Donor Contact Plan
The mother's milk of politics $$$$$$$

Campaign donations are the mother's milk of politics. This strategy will point you to the potential donors that are best for you. There are multiple groups and donor levels for your campaign. There are multiple ways for a new candidate to target donors $$$$$.

To be a creditable candidate in major election races you need to have a substantial financial fundraising report that lets the voters, and any opponent know you can raise the funds needed to compete. If you're running against an opponent that has been in a fundraising mode because they hold an elective office and unless you're in the same situation as your opponent, give yourself three months before the reporting date. Start your fundraising when you're sure you can report a substantive amount.

You can fund a run for a local government seat for very little.
- You substitute mailings with volunteers passing out flyers made on your home computer.
- More voter contact can be a neighborhood walk at least twice. Friends can do neighborhood coffee hours.
- Candidates running for State Senator and Representative can use these strategies. A mayoral candidate can do the same.
- Remember, "All politics is local".
- Look at each precinct and district as a separate and distinct race and part of the whole.
- This same strategy should hold in a U S Representative and U S Senate race.

This strategy will point you to locate & target 5-levels of donors. There are multiple ways for a new candidate to raise donations. This strategy is fast in locating & targeting the 5-levels of donor's best for you.

To be a creditable candidate in major election races you need to have a substantial financial fundraising report that lets the voters and any opponent know you can raise the funds needed to compete.

Run my Grassroots Campaign for a local government seat for little money.
- You can substitute mailings with volunteers passing out flyers
- Make your flyers on your home computer.
- Voter contact (ID) can be a neighborhood walk at least twice
- Friends can do neighborhood coffee hours.
- Candidates running for State Senator and Representative can use these strategies. A mayoral candidate can do the same.
- Remember "All politics is local". Look at each precinct as a separate and distinct target and part of the whole. This same strategy should hold in a Mayoral, U S Representative and U S Senate races.

There are multiple groups for your campaign

Start with the donors to the candidates who ran for the seat you are running for. Last election there was three candidates for the office in the party's primary. The winner went on to defeat in the General Election.

You enter the race and set the stage for the front-runner position. You're out of the gate early so everyone watches your moves. As long as you're on you're way in accomplishing the above strategies you can move to solicit donations.

Campaign Donors are Public Record

Campaign donations are public records. Find your Party's list of donors. Locate the donors who donated to the candidates that ran for the seat you are running for, the area your campaign falls within.

If you're running for Congressional seat find out the donors who contributed to all primary and general election candidates. If you're running for an open seat this group needs to be persuaded that you can win.

You must provide some evidence you can win. If you have followed the Grassroots Campaigning Strategies these strategies have made you a credible candidate and will help you obtain donations.

Qualify the donors that fall into the following level:
1. The maximum allowed
2. $500 -- $1000
3. $250 -- $499
4. $100 -- $249
5. $5.00 -- $99.00

Group 1, 2, & 3:
Send a letter to donors asking for their financial support. Write why you believe you will win the election and why you are running for the seat. Include donor cards and envelopes. You must follow-up with a telephone call. Large donors want to meet you before they donate.

Prepare Donor Cards with the following information:
Name_____ Address_____ Tel_____

Email Address_____

Amount_____ the donor gave to the last candidate for the office you are running for. Know the History of the donor.

Motivational reasons for potential donors
- The donors supports your issues and/or ideological concerns
- The donor feels a strong personal support for you
- Feels a strong opposition for your opponent
- Wants to be involved in a campaign
- Always donates to your party's candidates
- Believes that you can win

Group 4 & 5:
- Email and telephone soliciting may be best for budget reasons.
- Small donors may want to be involved and asking for their level of affordability will make them comfortable to respond. An Email and Telephone Campaign for small donors can be repeated every month and very week close to Election Day.

CHAPTER 2

I'll show you how to

Win Your Primary

- Cultivate your base
- Identify your Favorable & Volunteers to increase your vote.
- Your Undecided & Independents Vote
- Identify the Party's Base
- Target the Party's Faithful
- Survey to rate you & your opponent
- Target 5 groups of potential supporters
- Measure Persuadable & Performances
- Opposition Research the Opposition's Vote & Plan
- Know your Enemy
- Identify Your Donors
- GOTV a database of Favorables, volunteers and other potential supporters

Win your Primary

Know Your Enemy
- **Opposition Research**
- **ID the Opposition's Vote & Plan**

Register members of political Parties are considered the Party's base. The members who vote in the Party's primaries are the faithful primary voters.

Their choice, right or wrong is the candidate they want to lead the Party in the General Election. The perceptions (are political reality) marketed to the voters are what the voters expect from the winner of the Primary.

Democrat Candidates

The Democrat Primary winner defines where the voters want the winner to take the party forward.

The Registered Democrat Party's members are considered the Party's Base and the party's faithful vote in the Democrat Primaries. Their choice, right or wrong is the candidate they want to have on the ballot for the General Election.

The candidates in the primary could be a liberal, a conservative and a moderate. They must come together in order to win the General election and unit all members of the Party behind the nominee.

Example:

The incumbent is a left wing Democrat. The voter's last primary election selected him over his conservative opponent. The D-Base said they wanted to be represented by an extreme liberal. The question after the Primary; will the majority of the voters in the district elect the D-Base choice? The last General Election was so close that less then 1% gave the Democratic candidate a victory.

The Republican candidate was a moderate expected to run again. Polling has shown that 5% of voters have moved away from the extreme left, leaving the D-Base and the district voters ready for a change. The only way the Democrat can hope to hold the seat is to elect a moderate in the Democrat Primary. The forecast is the majority of the district voters have moved to the center. The General Election will define the all District's electorate.

The Open Seat
The incumbent Democrat candidate is not running for re election. An open seat situation almost always causes Party Primaries. Ask yourself the following questions:

- Do you have support of political and community leaders?
- Are you prepared to announce your campaign Headquarters & Staff?
- Is your Website up and ready for Declaration day?
- Are you the candidate to replace the incumbent?
- Are you the candidate who is or can be the unofficial spoke person for you're the people?

A political campaign must ask.
What are the negatives to an issue or any campaign strategy and tactic? Forget the intent, its all about perception.

Perception is Political Reality
The first candidate to announce his or her candidacy is the only candidate out of the gate. Thus, first is out in front. Grassroots campaigning strategies will help you stay in front.

Independent Candidate
The Independent Candidate must implement the strategies in my Grassroots-Campaigning Plan. Independent candidates start off behind. They look like the lone candidate without any major support. The first question everyone will ask:

1. "How much money can you raise"?
2. "How much will you right a check for?"

Its credibility you need and you have to demonstrate you have or can raise the money and have a solid organization. Independent candidates must overcome a party candidate by demonstrating a volunteer movement and imply you are the people's choice and voice.

Grassroots Campaign strategies, tactics and suggested materials will promote you and your campaign and bring aboard the supporters and volunteers you need to carry out your campaign agenda.

Voter Database
You started with your Name Recognition & Brand Campaign. Your second priority on the campaign trail was to get as many phone numbers and email addresses as possible.

The Headquarters staff needs to organize a database. All phone numbers and email addresses should be turned into HQ after each field event. When HQ receives the voter's information from the Advance Team, the In-house staff and volunteers enter the information into a database. From the list of potential supporters they can solicit Favorable and volunteers.

Candidates running in a primary must call their respective party's registered voters and ID the potential Favorable and encourage them to volunteer.

Email Addresses

Your campaign is always on a mission to get Email Addresses. This will assure that the voter is always in contact and informed of the campaigns events. Keep the voter in the loop, and keep the cost of voter contact to a minimum.

Picture for Emails

On the campaign trail have a photographer take pictures of you and the voters. Give the voters a card with the instruction to retrieve the picture. When the voter goes to the site he or she must enter their email address.

Enter the picture voters in your database to be called to be a volunteer. Call under the assumption that they are a Favorable.

Take all Prisoners

Take all prisoners is to accept everyone who is willing to support you. You do not have to bring them into your organization. Have your staff work with them and get the votes and networking they can deliver.

Support Groups

Have your support groups' leaders organize their members. Take no one for granted. Group leaders need to call every member and identify their position on the groups' candidate and identify the Favorable and ask them to join the campaign as a volunteer. Have all support groups organize an Email address list of all their members.

When you're in GOTV mode the last week of the election have members of the individual groups remind their members to vote for you. On the day of election have them call their members until voted.

Phone Bank Action

The *In-house* phone action is to identify the voters who have the greatest potential to support you. Your Favorable should be kept in the loop throughout the campaign. Your volunteers will come from this group.

When running in a large district, and you are able to hirer a phone bank to identify the voters in the target groups listed below, do it. This will bring a list of Favorable to identify as volunteers and donors. The Favorable are called by your volunteers from HQ and asked to become a volunteer member of the campaign. The Undecided are called to find out why they are undecided and what can "Candidate Smith" do to help you decide.

The *In-house* phones can get you multiple new Favorable from the Undecided and volunteers from the Favorable. Set your database for groups of positive, maybe, undecided and the opposition's voters. I like to keep track of the opposition voters on Election Day to see how they are voting in relation to the turnout and to the relation of my candidate's voters.

The Candidate & the Volunteer's Recruiting Sessions

Candidates spend a lot of hours calling and soliciting donations. They have to in order to move the donor to his campaign. However the candidate fails to spend sufficient time and effort getting volunteers interested in the workings of his campaign.

You should organize volunteer phone bank sessions where the volunteers on multiple phones call the Favorable and potential supporters. The callers should try to convince the voters to support the candidate and the Favorable to become a volunteer. The candidate should ask the reluctant voters to the Coffee Time so they can discuss any reservations the voter may have.

Moving from voter to voter, phone to phone, during this process the candidate should end the conversation with the voters and thank the new volunteer for joining the campaign and hopefully to meet them at the next Coffee Time if not before.

Call & ID Registered Voters:
1. The Favorable should be called to become a volunteer and to list their email address.
2. You want to invite all Favorable and undecided to the next Coffee Time with the candidate and tell them of the day and times every month the next one will be held.

Registered Party members are the Party's faithful and the Party's base. You must direct your campaign to your faithful primary voters first. Not all registered Party members faithfully vote in their primary. You have to identify the faithful primary voters who have the greatest potential to support you. I have selected five Groups for you to priorities.

Targeting the voters' is the process of research and analysis of voters' attitudes, based upon past voting behavior. You are concerned with finding the voters who have the greatest potential to vote for you.

Since Abe Lincoln organizing a campaign has become the science of political engineering. Abe knew the importance of making a list of who the voters will vote for on Election Day and make sure every potential favorable voter voted. Lincoln wrote, "…make a perfect list of voters and ascertain with certainty for which they will vote…and on Election Day see that every Whig gets to the polls. The Whig voter was a Lincoln favorable ID.

Targeting Your Voters

Five Target Groups of Potential Supporters

All new party registrations since the last election should be included in the following target groups.

Target Group # 1

The Registered Democrats who voted in both of the last two Democrat Primaries are your first target group. You have to assume they will vote in the next Democrat Primary. You must appeal to the faithful primary voters. You must meet and ask everyone you can for his or her vote. You must stay in contact by Email, U S Mail and telephone. The support of this #1 Democrat Base means you're the front-runner for the Primary and have the best chance to win the Primary. You want to wake up primary morning and know you have enough Favorable voters identified to win and the means to get them to the polls to vote.

Target Group # 2

The Registered Democrats who voted in the last Democrat Primary and not the previous Democrat Primaries are your 2nd target group.

Target Group # 3

The Registered Democrats who missed the last Democrat Primary, but voted in the previous Democrat Primary is your 3rd target group.

Target Group # 4

The Registered Democrats, who do not vote in Democrat Primaries, must be encouraged to vote in your primary. They will not unless they have a reason that is meaningful to them.

What may bring them out to vote is a political issue that they feel so strong about they have to vote against your opponent. A second reason is they know and really like a candidate. It's up to you to get them to like you. Primaries can be a popularity contest.

Target Group # 5

Find Independents and unaffiliated who voted in the last Democrat Primary and disaffiliated after voting.

The Democrat Primary voters who disaffiliated are more often then not Independent Democrats. It is unusual for an Independent Republican to vote in a Democrat Primary, they are crossovers and need a very good reason. The true Independents will vote anywhere, anytime and especially if they are angry at the status quo. In this group are the Favorable for your primary campaign, go get them.

Primaries are easier to target the voters who have the greatest potential to vote for you.

You can focus on the registered voters of your respective party and if need be the registered Independents. Survey and identify your Favorable & your potential supporters who may become volunteers.

To receive a ready survey response, ask the voters;
How do they your rate your opponent?

Excellent__ Good__ Fair__ Poor__ don't know__ Undecided__.

1. Voters who answer *"Poor"* are your best bet to list as a Favorable. Ask this voter to be a volunteer for your campaign. You should list all members of the household as a Favorable.

2. Voters who *"Don't know"* may be uninformed and need to be sent campaign literature and other persuasive actions. The more you reach out to them the best chance you will have to get their vote and find out their true position. Hopefully your opponent gives them less attention. Invite to "Coffee Time" may help you understand their reluctance.

3. The *"Undecided"* need to be pushed to you. But don't push too hard they may be your opponents vote and don't want to say so. An invite to Coffee Time may bring out their position.

4. *Fair* is a borderline position. The voter could be for your opponent. The caller should try to determine what the voter means by Fair.

Target the swing districts

Locate the precincts that have a voting history of swing voting during the past three elections. If the precinct votes for a political party one election or two, and then votes for the other political party this precinct should be a target for voter persuasion.

Another barometer is the change in the percentages. For example a candidate for the Republicans may have received 65% of the vote three elections past, then 55% the next election. The last election the candidate only received 51% of the turnout. This precinct is ready to swing. This precinct must be a target for a heavy voter contact.

Flood the above precincts with literature and signs. Do business walks and neighborhood walks. Find volunteers who live and work in the area to walk with you and introduce you to the voters.

Call the registered Independent voters and invite them to participate in the campaign and to stop in at a Coffee Time. Have your volunteers pledge to bring a new potential Favorable and volunteer to the campaign's headquarters Coffee Time every 4th Wednesday night from 6:30 to 8:00.

Measure the Persuadable & Performances

You need to receive the greatest return for your campaign efforts; determine the precincts that will return you the most votes for your campaign's efforts. Time is valuable and you need to watch your campaign expenses.

- 1st Target the precincts where you have the most Favorable IDs.
- 2nd Target the precincts where you have a racial relationship, if significant.
- 3rd Target the precincts where you have a nationality relationship, if significant.
- 4th Target the precincts where your Party has a tradition of heavy turnout.

Question:
1. Where are the precincts that you should spend more time, doing campaign Business Walks, Neighborhood Walks and Honks & Waves?
2. Where should you get your supporters out with VAC Packs to FF&N?

Answer: The precincts that have a high turnout performance and their performance's are a history of swing voting.

Example
In 2006 in precinct #1 the vote for the Senate Candidate was 2,000 votes more then the Congressional Candidate of the same party. The difference between the Congressional Candidate and the Mayoral Candidate in the same precinct was close. The voters approved of the Mayoral and Congressional candidates about equal. The same voters approved of the

Senate candidate 2,000 votes more then the Congressional candidate. This precinct has the possibility of 2,000 persuadable voters.

You will find precincts that are consistent in their voting habits over the past two and three elections. Their voting history is a prediction for the next election. Make your appearance in the precincts that have the greatest history of independent voting.

You need to know what the percentage of the voters will turnout to vote. History of the last two elections will give you one presidential election and one non presidential election. Therefore if you are running in a non presidential year you have to use the last two non presidential elections as a guide.

You should find the voters who voted in the last presidential election and missed the previous non presidential election. Those voters should be persuadable.

Fundraising

Campaign donations are the mother's milk of politics. This strategy will point you to the potential donors that are best for you. There are multiple groups and levels for your campaign. There are multiple ways for a new candidate to raise donations.

To be a creditable candidate in major election race you need to have a substantial financial fundraising report that makes notice to the voters and opponents that you can raise the funds needed to compete.

If you're running against an opponent that has been in a fundraising mode because and unless you're in the same situation as your opponent, give yourself three months before the reporting date. Start your fundraising when you're sure you can report a substantive amount the next reporting dates.

You can run my Grassroots-Campaign for local government seat for very little. You substitute mailings with volunteers passing out flyers made on your home computer. Your voter contact can be a neighborhood walk at least twice. Friends can do neighborhood coffee hours.
Candidates running for State Senator and Representative can use these strategies. A mayoral candidate can do the same. Remember, "All politics is local". Look at each district as a separate and distinct race and part of the whole. Grassroots will get you elected a U S Representative and U S Senate.

There are multiple donor groups for your campaign.
You enter the race and set the stage for Front-runner position. You're out of the gate early so everyone watches your moves. As long as you're on you're way in accomplishing the above strategies you can move to solicit donations.

Campaign Donors are Public Record
Campaign donations are public records. Find your Political Party's list of donors. Locate the donors who donate to the candidates that ran for the seat you are running for. Go to the area your campaign falls within. If you're running for Congressional seat find out the donors who contributed to all primary and general election candidates.

If you're running for an open seat this group needs to be persuaded that you can win. You must provide some evidence. You need to show that you are the better candidate. If you have followed Grassroots campaigning strategies 1 and 2 these strategies have made you a credible candidate and will help you obtain donations.

Qualify the donors that fall into the following level:
1. Maximum allowed
2. $500 -- $1000
3. $250 -- $499
4. $100 -- $249
5. $5.00 -- $99.00

Group 1, 2, & 3:
Send a letter to donors asking for their financial support. Write why you believe you will win the election and why you are running for the seat. Include donor cards and envelopes. You must follow-up with a telephone call.

Large donors want to meet you before they donate. It is best to start this fundraising campaign before you announce, if possible. If not then you have to be ready to move this tactic as soon as possible.

Prepare Donor Cards with the following information:
Name_____ Address_____ Tel_____

Email Address_____

Amount_____ the donor gave to the last candidate for the office you are running for. Include a personal, business and political history of the donor.

Motivation reasons for potential donors
1. Supports your issues and/or ideological concerns.
2. Feels a strong support for you.
3. Feels a strong opposition for your opponent.
4. Wants to be involved.
5. Always donates to party candidates.

Group 4 & 5:
Email and telephone soliciting may be best for budget reasons. Small donors want to be involved and asking for their level of affordability will make them comfortable to respond. An Email and Telephone Campaign for small donors can be repeated every month and every week close to Election Day.

The Republican Candidate

What holds true for Democrats holds true for Republicans.

The GOP Primary defines the GOP Party and where the voters want the winner to take the party forward.

Know Your Enemy
- Opposition research
- ID the Opposition's vote
- Locate Potential Opposition
- Deter the Opposition

Within the Republican and Democrat voters there are fiscal and social conservatives, liberals, moderates and extremist. You need to know and identify your voters and motivate them onto your campaign and vote them Election Day.

Republican Primary Campaign

The Registered Republicans are considered the R-Base. I define the Republicans who faithfully vote in their party's primaries as the Republican Faithful primary voters, especially who voted in the last two or more Republican Primaries. New Republican registrations accepted. The Republican Primary winner defines where the Party wants to go and have chosen the direction they want you and the Party to go. Once the primary voters have spoken so has the R-Base.

Example: The incumbent Republican is an extreme right winger. The voters in the last Primary election wanted him over his conservative opponent. The R-Base said they wanted to be represented by an extreme right representative not a Ronald Reagan conservative.

The question after the Primary; will the majority of the voters in the district's General Election except the Republican Primary's choice? The last General Election was so close that less then 1% gave the Republican candidate a victory.

The Democrat candidate was a moderate expected to run again. Polling has shown that 5% of voters have moved away from the extreme right, leaving the district voters ready for a change. The only way Republicans can hope to hold the seat is to elect a conservative and/or a moderate candidate in their Republican Primary.

The forecast is the majority of the district voters have moved to the center. The General Election will define the District's electorate and in all probability elect a candidate who can position himself in the center.

The Open Seat:

The Incumbent Democrat candidate is not running for re election. An open seat situation almost always causes a Party Primary. Be the first to announce for the open seat implement the 13 step front-runner campaign.

You must direct your campaign to your R-Base, the voters who voted in the last two Republican Primaries. You can usually count on them for the General Election but not in the primary.

Organize your Target Groups.

Registered Republicans who vote in the Primaries are the number one target group to ID.

Target Group # 1
The Registered Republicans who voted in both of the last two Republican Primaries are your first target group. You must first appeal to them for support. They will vote in the next Republican Primary. You must meet and ask everyone you can for his or her vote. You must stay in contact via Email letter, U S Mail and telephone.

The support of the majority of this # 1 R-Base will mean you're the front-runner. A survey of this R-Base that you are the Front-runner will support your campaign in numerous ways, especially in volunteers and donors. If you got it flaunt it.

Target Group # 2
The Registered Republicans who voted in the last DP and not the previous Republican Primaries are your 2nd target group. Who are the new voters?

Target Group # 3
The Registered Republicans who missed the last DP but voted in the previous Republican Primaries are your 3rd target group.

Target Group # 4
The remaining Registered Republicans who do not vote in the Republican Primary must be encouraged to vote in your primary. They will not unless they have a reason that is meaningful to them. What will bring them out to vote is a political issue that they feel so strong about they have to vote against one of the candidates. A second reason is they know and really like a candidate and are not happy with his opponent.

Target Group #5

Find Independents and unaffiliated who voted in the last Republican Primary and disaffiliated after voting.

The Independent Voters

The Independents & unaffiliated voters are Independent Democrats, Independent Republicans and the true Independent swing voters. In this target group are Favorable IDs for your primary campaign, which you will need for the General Election.

The Independent Republican Primary voter who disaffiliated is more often then not are Independent Republican. It is unusual for an Independent Democrat to vote in a Republican Primary. The true Independents will vote anywhere, if anything, they are angry at the status quo. In this target group are Favorable for your primary campaign, go get them.

1st Target the precincts where you have the most favorable IDs.
2nd Target the precincts where you have a racial relationship, if significant.
3rd Target the precincts where you have a nationality relationship, if significant.
4th Target the precincts where you have the most support and use your VAC Pack campaign.

Primaries are easier to target voters who have the greatest potential to vote for you. You can start with two groups:
- You're Party's registered voters
- You're Party's Base of faithful primary voters
- Registered Independents.

Target the swing districts

Locate the precincts that have a voting history of swing voting during the past three elections. If the precinct votes for a political party, one election or two and then votes for the other political party they should be a target for voter contact.

Another barometer is the change in the percentages. For example a candidate for the republicans may have received 65% of the vote three elections past, then 55% the next election. The last election the candidate only received 51% of the turnout. This precinct is ready to swing. This precinct must be a target for a heavy voter contact.

Flood the above precincts with literature and signs. Do business walks and neighborhood walks. Find volunteers that know voters in these areas to promote you and introduce you to voters. Call registered Independent voters and invite them to participate in the campaign and to stop in at a coffee hour.

Volunteers are encouraged to pledge to bring a new voter to a weekly campaign's headquarters coffee hour every 4th Wednesday night from 6:30 to 8:00.

CHAPTER 3

I'll show you how to

GOTV Election Week & Day

- ID faster, more actuate.
- Motivate Volunteers & Favorable.
- Light up the district for Election.
- GOTV Favorable IDs
- Checker Plan to Win
- Tracking with Voter Par Count
- True Election Day situation Demonstrates how
- GOTV was accomplished to save the Primary Election.

GOTV Election Day & Week

GOTV Election Week
- ID faster more actuate
- Motivate Volunteers & Favorable
- Light up the district for Election

GOTV Election Day
- Vote Favorable IDs
- Checker Plan to win
- Tacking with Voter Par Count
- My true story of how I directed a Senatorial Primary Election in the last 3 hours to save a win. This is what it's all about…

Election Day
You need to wake up on Election Day morning with more than 50% Favorable IDs to win. You must have the volunteer teams to encourage the Favorable to get to the voting booths and cast their ballot for you. Every Favorable contacted the week of the election must be called on Election Day until voted. Using the Checker Plan will keep you updated as to who has voted. You must know if your voters are voting par with the expected turnout. You need runners to carry the voting behavior to HQ for volunteers to keep track of the Favorables' voting.

You must have volunteer teams of checkers to monitor the voters and greeters at all the polling locations to remind the voters to vote for you. A significant number of undecided voters can be impressed at the last minute before entering the voting booth.

GOTV
Identify the voters who will elect you
On the Campaign Trail & In-house Phone Bank

You have accomplished the process or in the process of implementing your GOTV plan. Review the following voter contact strategies for election week & Election Day to see what you have accomplished and what needs to be done.

1. In #1 did you build your Brand and go on the campaign trail to get as many phone numbers and email addresses as possible. Every voter met on the trail was a potential Favorable supporter & volunteer

2. In #2 you organized to win your In House staff & volunteers. They got on the Phone Bank and Identified Favorable & potential volunteers.

3. In #3 Win Your Primary you did a complete ID of your vital target groups to win the election.

4. The survey of voters during #3 Win your Primary identified your Favorable, volunteers and potential Favorable. You have determined who your negatives are.

5. Your campaign must devote the week of the General Election to remind every potential Favorable to vote.

6. In the process volunteers are recruiting more volunteers to guarantee you have more than enough volunteers and Favorable to win.

7. As a result of the above, you should have a bank of positive Favorable and potential Favorable for GOTV. Remember you need to wake up Election Day with a database of 51% Favorable of the expected turnout.

8. The week of the General Election your Phone Bank & Emails are in action campaigning to get out the vote for Election Day.

9. The Campaign has a database of voters for GOTV:
    -   Favorable

    This goes without saying; you must get them to the polls.
    -   Potential Supporters

    This group is the voters who you and your volunteers believe may vote for you if you encourage them to vote.

10. Volunteers

    Volunteers are the ones who will keep calling the Favorable, until they have voted. They are the loyal supporters who will find the voters who have the greatest opportunity to vote for you when you need them most on Election Day.

Every voter meeting on the campaign trail should have been asked for their phone number & email address. The Favorable expressing interest in the candidate should have been encouraged to join the campaign and become a volunteer. The most enthusiastic volunteers are the ones that walk in or call HQ. Give them an assignment before they leave the building.

Your volunteers with VAC (volunteer action committee) for FF&N (friends, family & neighbors) should be out trying to persuade voters and reminding the Favorable to vote Election Day.

VOLUNTEERS * VOLUNTEERS * MORE VOLUNTEERS
"Voice of the People"

There is a movement going on!
It's a Grassroots Movement it's the *"Voice of the People"*

Grassroots campaigning is the most affective way to attract Volunteers. The Volunteer movement is and of itself persuasive to the Independent and undecided voters. The perception; voters are energized for the candidate. The campaign is more street & HQ active than your opponents. It makes the statement "people over politics." "Perception is political reality" Grassroots campaigns are the "Voice of the People".

Voter Contact started on the campaign trail to get as many phone numbers and email addresses as possible. Supporters found, became the Favorable and from them come the all important volunteers.

This Grassroots Campaign is focused on getting the biggest percentage of the Favorable to become a volunteer to get more volunteers to bring home your vote Election Day.

All phone numbers and E-mail addresses should have been turned into HQ after each field event. The HQ Phones contacted the voters and identified them as potential Favorable and solicited volunteers.

The E-mails are also set up for voters to be subscribers to the candidate's E-mail Letters to keep them in the loop. There is no voter contact less expensive than E-mails to encourage voters to donate, become a volunteer and promote your election.

Support Groups' GOTV
Support groups should be organized to execute their inner group GOTV.
Have your support groups organize an E-mail address list of their members. When in GOTV mode, group members should participate in a GOTV group effort.

- The initial goal of the group's callers is to get a commitment from the members that they will vote on Election Day for you.
- Group members should ask all their group members to join the group's volunteers for GOTV.
- Group members should call FF&N to ask them to vote for you.
- Support groups should encourage their members to participate in the Coffee Times with the candidate every 4th Wednesday every month and to bring a potential supporter.
- With the larger groups, have a designated Coffee Time with the candidate. Special attention goes a long way.
- Group members can expand the VAC Pack distribution by encouraging members to distribute them to FF&N.
- The follow-up effort to all members of the group should be active the last week of the election.
- The day of election, all members should be called all day until they're voted.

- It's only a false roomer that voters will get mad and as a result, it could affect their vote if you call them too much. Just get them to vote and you got their vote.

VAC Pack for FF & N

You gave volunteers five or ten VAC Packs for FF&N and asked them to bring at least one voter to the coffee hours. This resulted in more volunteers who took home VAC Packs and so on and on.

Election week is the time to have every supporter & volunteer to get out VAC Packs to FF&N. All supporters when asked will hand out what they feel they can. If they can come in to HQ, it will demonstrate they are energized. If not, you must have the VAC Packs delivered to them.

The VAC Pack should contain about 6 campaign items.
Be creative!

1. Slim Jim Handouts and/or 3-Fold Flyers.
2. Letter to voters from volunteers asking for their support (Create a form letter and have the volunteers write in the voter's name and signed by the volunteer).
3. Stickers–Lapel and Bumper.
4. A Sample ballot of the candidate's position on the ballot.
5. Any other materials that will help the voter decide for the candidate.

The General Election

**You must direct your campaign to your
Party's Base & Independents**

The Registered Democrats, Republicans and Independents/Unaffiliated are the target groups for the Phone Bank, to identify the voters who have the greatest potential to support you, and to solicit for becoming a volunteer.

The new game in town is to run in the 3rd column as an Independent Democrat or Independent Republican. It has some value and in the right situation can be a win.

Potential Support Groups

Target Group # 1

The Registered who voted your Party's Primaries are your first target group. You must appeal to them for support. You can usually count on them for the General Election. You must ask everyone you can for his or her vote and to be a volunteer. Asking a person to be a volunteer even before you ask them to support you is a compliment. You gave them respect, and told them they are valuable to your election.

Call the Party's Base, the registered party members who voted in the last two and three Party Primaries and find new volunteers. You captured the majority of voters in the primary; therefore you have more then 50% Favorables in this database. The rest of the primary voters are for the most part yours. Send emails, have volunteers call and you will find more volunteers for your campaign.

Target Group # 2

The registered new voters for your party and new registered Independents must be targeted. New voters are a good bet to rally into your campaign.

Target Group # 3

The Registered Independent voters are potential Favorable and volunteers for your campaign, go get them.

- 1st Target the precincts where you have the most Favorable IDs.
- 2nd Target the precincts where you have a racial relationship, if significant.
- 3rd Target the precincts where you have a nationality relationship, if significant.
- 4th Target the precincts where your Party has a tradition of Favorable.

If you are running as an Independent-Democrat or Independent-Republican, the

Independents are first and the registered Party voters you associate your label with are your second target. Eliminate the registered opposition Party voters who consistently vote in their respective Party's primaries. You have a better chance with the voters who do not vote in primaries.

Phone Bank

Volunteers should call and identify the voters who have the greatest potential to support you. Your Favorable should have been kept in the loop throughout the campaign. Your volunteers will come from this group.

When running in a large district, and you are able to hirer a phone bank to identify the voters in the target groups listed in #3 Win you're Primary --do it. This will bring a list of voters who have the greatest potential to vote for you.

- From this list the Favorable are called by your volunteers from your HQ and asked to become a volunteer.
- The Undecided are called by your volunteers to find out why they are undecided and what can "candidate Smith" do to help you decide.
- The volunteer callers will get you multiple new voters and volunteers. Place the voters in response groups such as positive, maybe, undecided, no.

The Phone Bank Election Week

Survey to find more Favorable & Volunteers
- Democrat Primary candidates should survey Registered Democrats and Registered Independents.

- Republicans Primary candidates, should survey Registered Republicans and Registered Independents.

This survey will get right to the answers you need:
- Ask the voters if they will vote on Election Day.
- If the answer is Yes __ then ask for their vote for your candidate.
- If the answer is Yes__ then ask them to be a volunteer.
- The "Undecided" need to be sent campaign literature and other persuasive actions. Ask them for their Email Address, and send them some information about the candidate that they are undecided about.
- During the week of the election and on Election Day the candidate can participate in the calls to potential Favorable for volunteering and to lock in their vote.

HQ Phone Bank
- Survey voters on the candidate's political party's registered voting list.
- Survey the voters on the registered Independent voting list.
- ID Favorable from the list of the candidate's party's registered voters.
- Solicit volunteers from the Favorable.
- Use the Favorable list for your Donor campaign.
- Prepare the Favorable list for GOTV.
- The Favorable, Unfavorable & Undecided.
- You want as many Email Addresses as possible.
- You want to invite all Favorable and Undecided to attend the next "Coffee Time" with the candidate.
- Remember to tell them the day, and times of every month for coffee.

Target the Swing Districts
Locate the precincts that have a voting history of swing voting during the past three elections. If the precinct votes for a political party, one election or two and then votes for the other political party, they should be a priority target for your survey.

The last two weeks of the campaign flood the above precincts with literature and signs. Do business and neighborhood walks. Find volunteers that know voters in these areas to promote you and introduce you to voters. You want to ready them for a positive response during your final persuasion calls.

Call registered Independent voters and invite them to participate in the campaign and to stop in at Coffee Time. Every volunteer is encouraged to bring a new voter to the campaign's headquarters Coffee Time every 4th Wednesday night from 6:30 to 8:00.

Measure the Persuadable
Measure the Performances

You need to receive the greatest return for your campaign efforts; determine the precincts that will return you the most votes for your campaigning.

- Where are the precincts you should spend time doing Business and Neighborhood Walks and Honks & Waves?
- Where are the precincts you should get your supporters out with VAC Packs to FF&N?

The swing precincts and the precincts where you have a large voter approval should be your targets.

In 2006, precinct #1, the vote for the Senate candidate was 2,000 votes more then the congressional candidate of the same party. The difference between the congressional candidate and the Mayoral candidate in the same precinct was close. The voters liked the Mayoral and congressional candidates about equal. The same voters liked the Senate candidate 2,000 votes more then the congressional candidate. This precinct has the possibility of 2,000 persuadable voters.

You will find precincts that are consistent in their voting habits over the past two and three elections. Their voting history is a prediction for the next election. Make your appearance in the precincts that have the greatest history of independent voting.

You need to know what the percentage of voters will turnout Election Day. History of the turnout for the last two elections will give you one presidential election and one non presidential election. If you are running in a non presidential year you have to use the last two non presidential elections as a guide.

You should find the voters who voted in the last presidential election and missed the previous non presidential election. Those voters have the potential to be persuaded to vote and for you.

GOTV

- GOTV Get is about identifying your Favorable and getting them voted on Election Day.
- You must have the ability to make sure they are prodded and pushed until voted.
- You must have the ability to monitor the voting behavior Election Day, to know what your vote is doing in relation to the turnout.
- You must have a bank of voters who have the possibility to rescue your campaign on Election Day. (My true story will reveal this)
- Most important, you must have the volunteers to get the job done.

Voter Check System

The Voter Check System will give you the ability to vote every Favorable and increase the candidate's votes on Election Day. This is your edge to win.

Voter Par Count

The Voter Par Count is focused on tracking the Favorable voting behavior on Election Day. What is the percentage of the candidate's Favorable IDs who have voted in relation to the turnout at any given time on Election Day?

The Last Night of the Campaign

It's the last night of the campaign and you are meeting with your staff and volunteers. If you and your organization have accomplished all or what was necessary of the strategies in Grassroots-Campaigning, you know where you stand with the voters and what race position to victory you're at.

The most important question is; "Do we have enough Favorable to win tomorrows election?" A "YES" means that everyone starts to call all the Favorable and remind them to vote tomorrow.

The Field Operation

Put up signs all around the polling locations. Ge the candidates name in front of the voters on the way to the polls and at the polls. Have your Greeters ready to meet the voters at the polling locations with a card showing where you are on the ballot.

The Smaller Districts Candidates

If you're running in a small district where you have walked the district and charmed the voters twice, you should have enough Favorable to win. That is more than 50% of the voters expected to turnout. In the larger districts you should have made sure that your name recognition and voter contact campaign was very effective.

Election Eve

The election eve meeting is a tell all where you will be on Election Day.

If you have more than enough volunteers and staff for your GOTV Election Day Strategies, then you're in good steed. More important, if you have enough Favorable to win and a ready GOTV – YOU WILL WIN THE ELECTION.

* Volunteers for Telephone Callers.
* Volunteers for Poll Greeters.
* Volunteers for Poll Checkers.
* Volunteers for HQ & Poll Runners.
* Volunteers for Drivers.
* Volunteers for Sign Distributors near polling locations and major intersections.
* Volunteers for Election Day Literature Distribution.

GOTV Election Day
- GOTV: Vote the Favorable ID.
- The Voter Check Plan, will give you the ability to vote every Favorable and increase the candidate's votes on Election Day, the edge to win.
- GOTV is focused on tracking the Favorable voting behavior on Election Day by using the Voter Par Count.
- GOTV Election Day is to monitor the voters and to assure the candidate's Favorable are voting at a rate that will bring victory to the candidate.
- VOTER PAR COUNT: the percentage of the candidate's Favorable IDs who have voted in relation to the turnout out at any given time on Election Day!
- The more volunteers target and network the voters, the more successful Election Day GOTV.

Volunteers identified the Favorable and their expected time to vote. You should have identified more Favorable than what you believe your opponent will vote and at least 51% of the expected turnout.

A Voting Situation
The Polling locations open at 7:00 am. Polling officials will have the voting list. The voter will give his name to an election official. The official will certify the voter. A volunteer for the candidate is seated near. Upon hearing the person's name (Adam, Charles) a volunteer for the candidate will mark the name of the person as voted. At approximately 9:15 a volunteer runner for the candidate will pick up the list of who voted. This will go on every hour all day.

Volunteers at HQ will check off the candidate's Favorable who have voted and how many have voted in relation to the turnout. Keeping track of the Favorable informs the GOTV staff who voted and who to call to vote. Volunteers should start calling the candidate's Favorable who have not voted by 10:30 a. m.

What is the percentage of the candidate's Favorable who have voted in relation to the turnout at any given time on Election Day?

Undecided IDs should be marked as a possible vote for the candidate or a negative vote. It is up to the caller to determine from the conversation if it is possible to get the vote. This group is not counted in when the Favorable IDs. This group becomes important when in the closing hours of the day when the race is to close to call. At this time the volunteers must go to the list of voters who have the greatest potential to vote for you and determine if the voter will vote for you. If so the volunteer then encourages the voter to go to the polls and vote.

A True Election Day Situation Demonstrates how GOTV was accomplished to save the Election.

GOTV and Voter Par Won the Election!
How it works

Sandy Hanaway was the unendorsed candidate in the Democrat Primary for State Senator for Senate District 33 in Cumberland Rhode Island. This was a hard fought contest because the primary winner was expected to win easily in the General Election in thirty days.

She and her volunteers had walked the district twice. Volunteers were greeting the voters at the polls and promoting Sandy, myself included. Volunteers had all the polling locations covered. They were doing the Voter Check count and in the early voting hours, Sandy's IDs were turning out to vote.

The primary win against a popular opponent and a well oiled political machine would be an upset. Our GOTV pre Election Day effort had identified enough Favorable IDs for a Sandy victory. I returned to Sandy's HQ at 2:00 pm to find everyone in high spirits with typical anticipated Election Day victory smiles. Our tracking of IDs showed that Sandy was holding steady as her IDs were voting at no less then 35% of the total turnout.

GOTV on Election Day is focused on voting the favorable IDs, by tracking the voter's behavior on Election Day, and using the Voter Par Count; the percentage of the candidate's Favorable IDs, who have voted in relation to the turnout at any given time on Election Day?

I was hoping to be closer to 50%, 35% was too close. The opposition was not doing any better and the Undecided were voting heavy. In small voting districts, voters will ID Undecided so as not to let their neighbors know who they will vote for. You can always depend on the endorsed party voters and the anti party voters to take a stand. You have to get everyone of your voters to the polls or risk losing by a failed turnout. When the 4 o'clock sheets came in, tallying of the turnout in relation to Sandy's IDs found that Sandy's position dropped from 35% to 32%. I was concerned. We were having the voter turnout list brought into HQ every hour. At the 5 o'clock count her Favorable voting had dropped to 30%. The 6 o'clock count of 29% told me that her victory was failing. Her voters were staying home. The last three counts showed her Favorable voting had dropped 4% in three hours. Her voters needed to be encouraged to get to the polls.

Sandy had canvassed the district by phone went door to door and had plenty of IDs to win. What was missing was a Phone Bank calling Sandy's Favorable to remind them we needed their vote to win.

Her volunteers had worked day and night and put their hearts into winning. They did not want to hear from me, a political operative from another city, that their candidate was in a losing mode three hours before the polls close.

Reluctantly, I expressed my fears to everyone that Sandy's numbers were dropping and that she would lose unless we reversed this trend. We had to get the rest of her Favorable to vote. The volunteers were unsure of my evaluation.

One woman with a long history of political campaigns shouted that she believed Sandy will win. "I believe Sandy will win. I know the voters of this town." she said angrily. I was the outsider and she knew better then me. I shouted back in defense that "my figures don't lie". As I looked around I was standing alone. I had burst everyone's bubble.

The 7 o'clock count showed the number of Favorable voting had dropped to 28.3 of the turnout. At this point, everyone got concerned, and Sandy asked me what I though she should do. I told her I needed a place with five phones and five volunteers to call her Favorable, to express how much Sandy needed their vote. Volunteers jumped at the chance to get on the phones to save the election. We went to her office phones and proceeded to call 200 Favorable.

We started with the positive Favorable and then called the Maybe IDs. In one precinct, she had more than 80 Favorable who had not voted. We told the voters how close the race was and ultimately the winner could be decided by their vote. Besides that heavy burden, we offered rides and whatever was needed for them to vote. We dealt very cautious with the Maybe IDs. If they seemed to be a potential vote for Sandy we pushed for them to vote, if not we backed off. We called right up to 8:45 pm. just 15 minutes to the polls closing, because most voters live near their
Polling location, they could get to the polls on time.

After the polls closed, volunteers and supporters met at a local restaurant, waiting for results that our runners would bring in from the polling locations. Upon my arrival, I was greeted with harsh words from David Cruise, who resigned from the Senate seat Sandy was running for, to be Chief of Staff for the newly elected Governor of RI.. Cruise became my new boss as I joined the Governors Office as a Policy Analyst. Election Day jitters can shorten anyone's fuse. Everyone was bottled up and ready to cry in defeat.

Sandy had done her homework and her volunteers had covered all the bases. If her Favorable turned out she could absorb her opponent's late GOTV turnout. By 9:30 pm. all but one precinct had reported in, and Sandy was losing by 37 votes. Cruise was taking the count and writing the numbers on the board as they came in. Waiting for the last precinct, and trailing by 37 votes was very emotional and stressful for all of us.

Cruise walked over to me and said, "I'm going to cry." I replied, "We can still pull it out. This is the precinct with more than 80 Favorable that had not voted when we went to the phones. If they voted as promised we can pull it out." I could see a spark of hope ignite in David, as he continued to pace back and forth.

The only thing that would prove I was right, and leave me in good graces with everyone, would be a very close win for Sandy. I did not want to see what defeat would bring. There are no hero's in defeat. I prayed that we pulled out a win by our 11th hour GOTV effort.

A few minutes later David asked, "What are your figures again?" I assured him we had contacted more than 80 Favorable in the precinct we was waiting for.
Another positive factor when we went to the phones, Sandy's Favorable in the precinct were voting better than 50% in relation to the turnout. Sandy should win this precinct, but can she overcome the 37 vote deficit plus one to win. I believed at that point she could do it, I could see the renewed sense of hope I gave Cruise.

A few minutes later the runner came in with the count. We made up the 37 vote deficit and had enough left over to give Sandy a 17 vote win. Thus proving that GOTV and the Voter Par Count is a win.

To Emphasize & Remind you of Election Day Visibility
When the campaign switches over to a GOTV on Election Day volunteers make the candidate's name, picture and literature visible in front of the voters all day long.

Election Day visibility may be the last stratagem that gets the vote. It places the candidate's name and picture in front of the voters all day long. Place signs on the way to the polls and at polling locations. Volunteers greeting the voters at polling locations wearing the candidate's stickers, holding a sign and handing out sample ballots with the candidate's name and where the candidate's is on the ballot, may get that undecided vote.

A large percentage of voters go to the polls undecided. Have your volunteers target voters who seem to lean towards you, they may be the group who will bring you across the finish line in a tight race.

* Volunteers for Telephone Callers
* Volunteers for Poll Greeters
* Volunteers for Poll Checkers
* Volunteers for HQ & Poll Runners
* Volunteers for Drivers
* Volunteers for Sign Distributors near polling locations and major intersections
* Volunteers for Election Day Literature Distribution

For More Information or Coaching
A Personal Campaign Coach!
Joe will Analyze & Advise your Campaign & Guide you to Victory! For more information e-mail GrassrootsCampaigning@Yahoo.com